TROMBONE/EUPHONIUM

TEAM BRASS

RICHARD DUCKETT

REPERTOIRE

International Music Publications Limited

Edited by Philip Evry and Stephen Clark
Cover Design: Ian Barrett / Peter White
Cover Photography: Ron Goldby
Production: Peter White / Stephen Clark
Reprographics: Positive Colour Ltd.
Instruments photographed by courtesy
of Vincent Bach International Ltd.

First Published 1990
Reprinted 1993

© International Music Publications Limited
Southend Road, Woodford Green,
Essex IG8 8HN, England

TEAM BRASS REPERTOIRE: Trombone / Euphonium
ISBN 0 86359 715 7 / Order Ref: 17163 / 215-2-589

INTRODUCTION

TEAM BRASS *Repertoire Books* contain a wide variety of music in popular styles, including T.V., Film, Classics, Folk and Jazz. The *Repertoire Books* have been specially designed to supplement the TEAM BRASS *Tutor Series*, and each repertoire piece is appropriate to a particular level of attainment in the corresponding TEAM BRASS *Tutor*.

Many of the repertoire pieces are arranged for ensemble. These are basically duets, to which can be added independent (and inessential) third and fourth parts. This book includes 9 such arrangements for trombone trio, which may also be played as duets by omitting the lowest part. In addition, all these pieces may be played by a mixed brass ensemble, using the relevant parts contained in the *F Horn*, *Trumpet* and *Brass Band Books*. The optional fourth parts for use with this book and others in the TEAM BRASS series, together with a conductor's score, are provided in the *Supplement*.

Several pieces of jazz have been included, and these can be used as a basis for improvisation — hints are provided on pages 4 and 5. For ease of reading, the early jazz pieces are given a straightforward rhythmic notation, viz. ♩ ♩ ♩ rather than, say ♫ , ♪♩ . Some suggested rhythmic interpretations are supplied in brackets.

The following symbol has been used to provide an immediate visual identification:

 An ensemble arrangement with supplementary parts in other TEAM BRASS *Repertoire books*.

There is an index of titles on page 32.

Jazz improvisation

The word 'improvisation' means that you have to make up your own music as you go along. You might have already done this, perhaps during your warm-up. One of the easiest ways, to begin with, is to make up music using a few notes only, for example:—

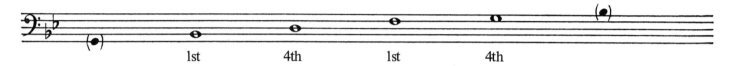

1st	4th	1st	4th

This is called a 'Quadratone' because it consists of only four notes — B♮, D, F and G which can all be played in the first and fourth positions. The idea is to use these notes to make up some quite short phrases, using jazz rhythms. Here are four examples to start you off. If you're not sure of the rhythms, ask your teacher to play them first, then play them yourself by ear:—

1)

2)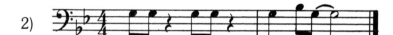

3)

4)

In 'Swing' time note lengths are varied, so that ♩♩ and ♩.♪ both tend to be played as ♩ ♪ .

Ex. (4) above, played with a swing, might go something like this:—

Of course, it would rarely be printed like that — it's much too difficult to read!

Not all popular music is intended to be 'swung'. Rock and Latin American rhythms, for instance, are usually played 'straight' (keeping to the printed note-lengths). It's up to you to learn to play both ways, so you can choose the style you think is right for any particular piece.

You might now try to vary the notes, or the rhythms, until you have built up quite a large catalogue of short phrases. Some short phrases can be put together to make longer ones. Next, try playing your phrases over the 12-bar blues sequence below. Listen carefully to how they fit (or don't fit!) with the keyboard. Change your notes if they do not match the chords:—

Accompaniment for piano or electronic keyboard on JAZZ ROCK setting.

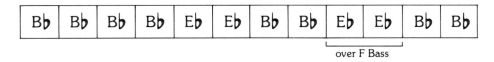

B♭	B♭	B♭	B♭	E♭	E♭	B♭	B♭	E♭	E♭	B♭	B♭

over F Bass

When you have gained some confidence in your ability to improvise, try introducing it into one of the jazz pieces in this book, like *When the saints go marching in,* or *Don't sit under the apple tree.*

Get together with a group of friends (for example, trumpet, trombone, electronic keyboard and drums), play through the piece twice, then take turns to improvise over the chord sequence. Finally, all play the piece through again to make a rousing finish.

You can expand your improvisation within the key of B♭ by adding some 'blues' notes. The new scale will look like this:—

Blues notes

You can use a mixture of scales if you wish. The really important thing is to listen to yourself in relation to the chord sequence. Sometimes your notes will grate against the chords — this is called 'dissonance' in music. Controlled dissonance is a very important part of jazz, and it takes quite a lot of experience to learn how to use it in a really effective way. To help yourself, record the 12-bar chord sequence (above) and spend many practice sessions experimenting with improvisation.

You will also find it helpful to listen to records of the all-time great brass jazz musicians. There are many to choose from, but one of the best was LOUIS ARMSTRONG. You will find his recordings in any reputable record shop.

When the saints go marching in

Traditional

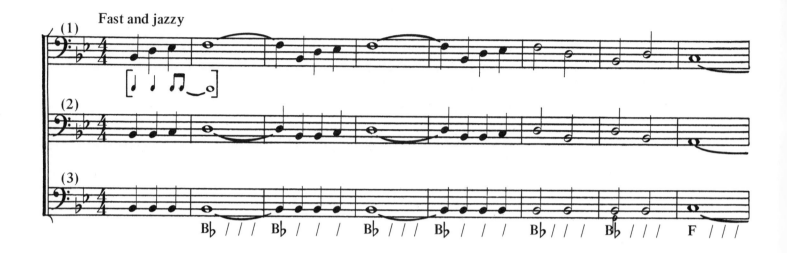

For improvisation, the chord sequence (above) may be used. The following more varied sequence will also fit this tune:—

Accompaniment for electronic keyboard on JAZZ ROCK.

B♭	B♭	B♭	B♭	B♭	B♭	F	F
B♭	B♭7	E♭	E♭m	B♭	C7 | F7	B♭	B♭

Ode to joy

LUDWIG VAN BEETHOVEN
(1770-1827)

Allegro assai

He's got the whole world in his hands

Traditional

Jolly

Don't sit under the apple tree (With anyone else but me)

Words and Music by LEW BROWN,
CHARLIE TOBIAS and SAM H STEPT

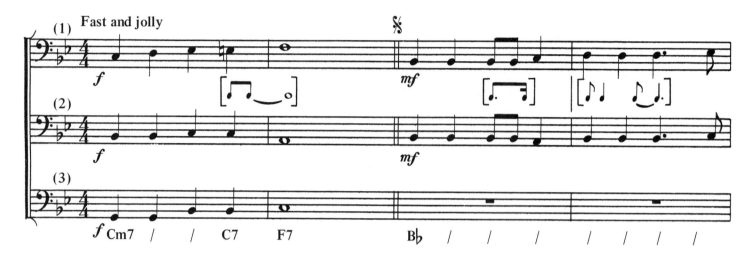

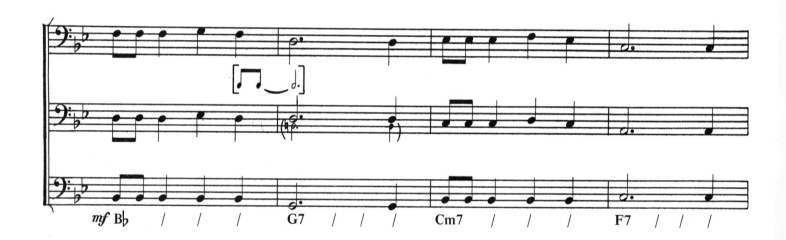

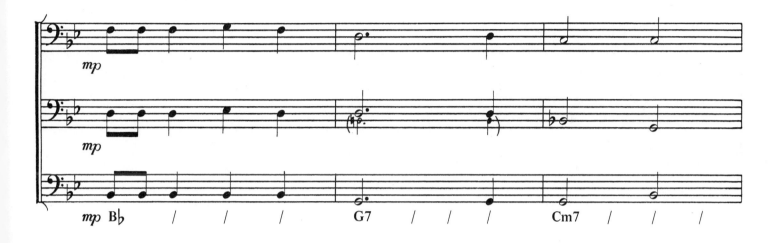

D.S. (ad lib)

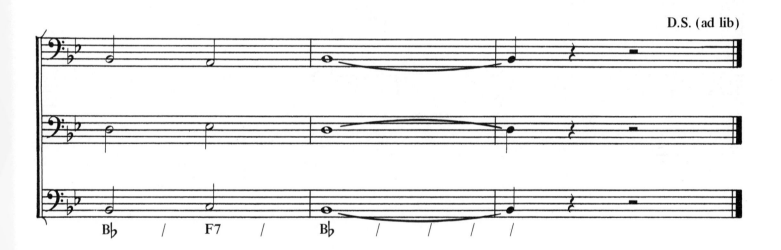

For improvisation, the chord sequence (above) may be used. Vary it, if you wish, by using the following sequence:-

Accompaniment for electronic keyboard on JAZZ ROCK.

B♭	B♭	B♭	B♭	F7	F7	B♭	B♭ F7

B♭	B♭	Fm(6)	G7	C7	F7	B♭	B♭

Kum-ba-ya

Traditional

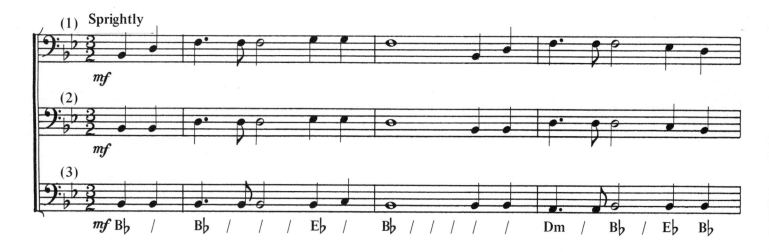

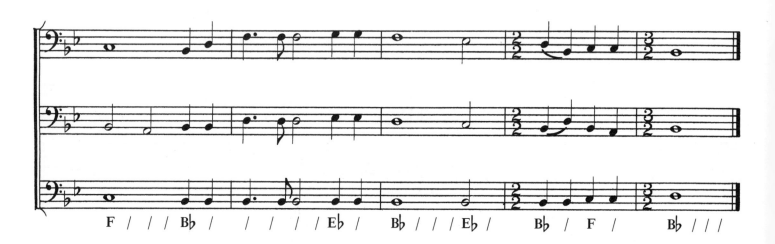

© 1990 International Music Publications, Woodford Green, Essex, IG8 8HN.

God save the Queen

Traditional

© 1990 International Music Publications, Woodford Green, Essex, IG8 8HN.

Down by the riverside

Traditional

Bouncy 4

Barcarolle

JACQUES OFFENBACH (1819-1880)

Andante

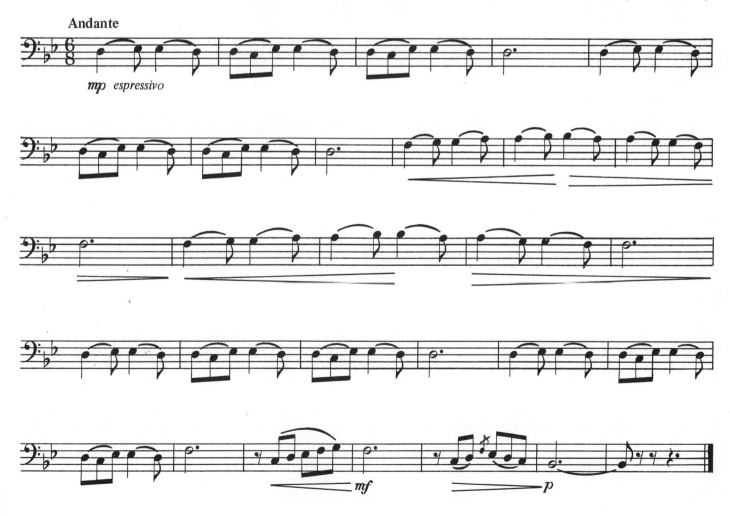

Old Mac's jazz

Traditional

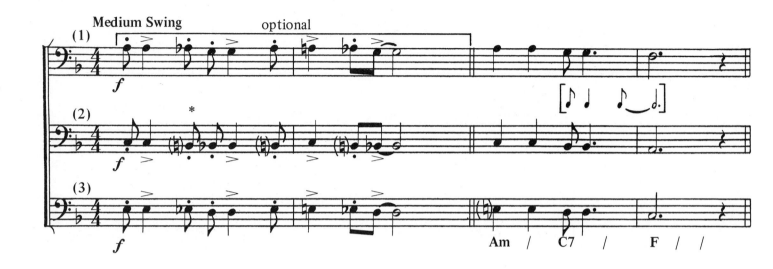

* B♮ can be played on euphonium or bass trombone, otherwise play B♭

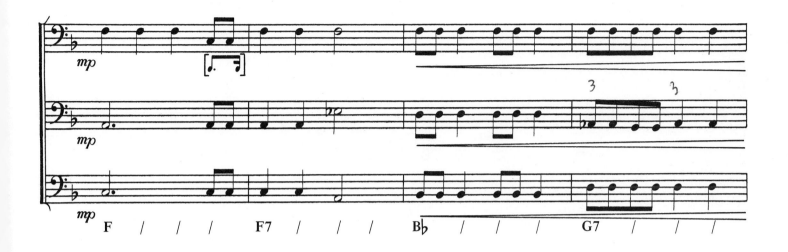

This scale can be used as a basis for improvisation on the above chord sequence:

Joy to the world

GEORGE FRIDERIC HANDEL (1685-1759)

Da Capo or
Dal Segno (ad libitum)

16

Introduction to 'Blue Danube'

JOHANN STRAUSS (1804-1849)

Very slow waltz

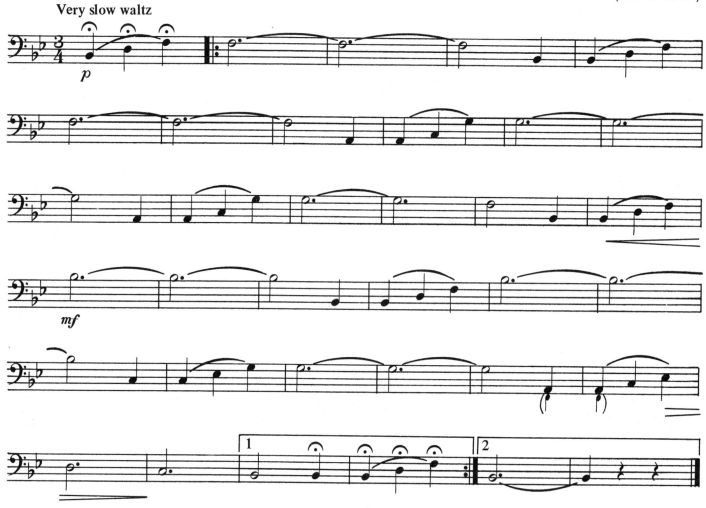

Morning has broken

Traditional

Happily

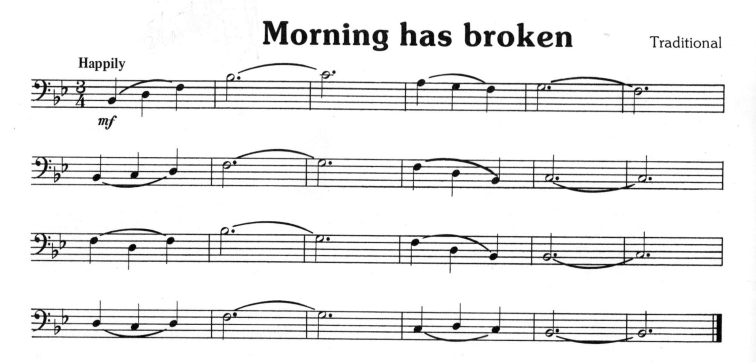

Over the rainbow

Words by E Y HARBURG
Music by HAROLD ARLEN

Brass suite

TIELMAN SUSATO (–c. 1561)

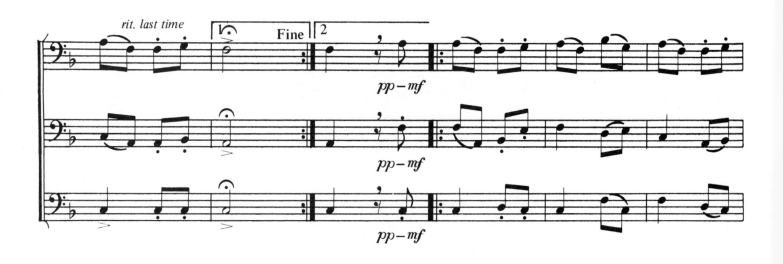

Dallas

JERROLD IMMET

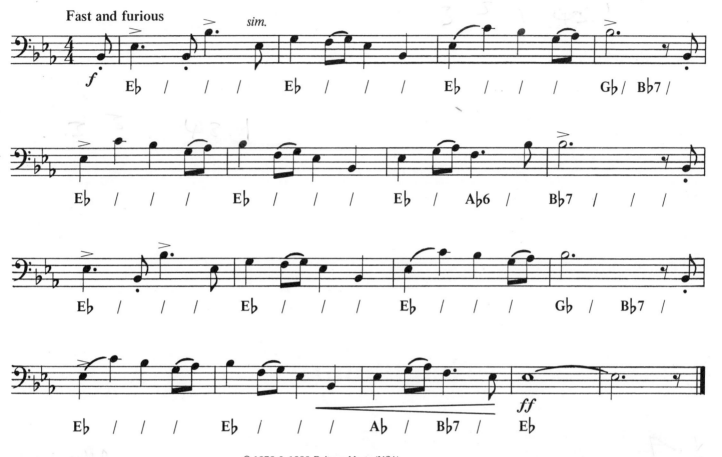

God rest ye merry, gentlemen

Traditional

Theme from 'New World' Symphony

ANTONIN DVOŘÁK (1841-1904)

Neighbours

Words and Music by
TONY HATCH and JACKIE TRENT

Scarborough Fair

Traditional

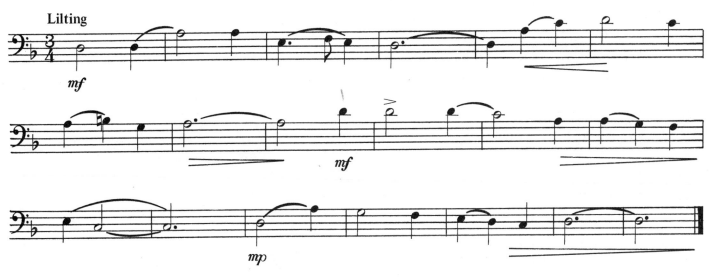

The pink panther

HENRY MANCINI

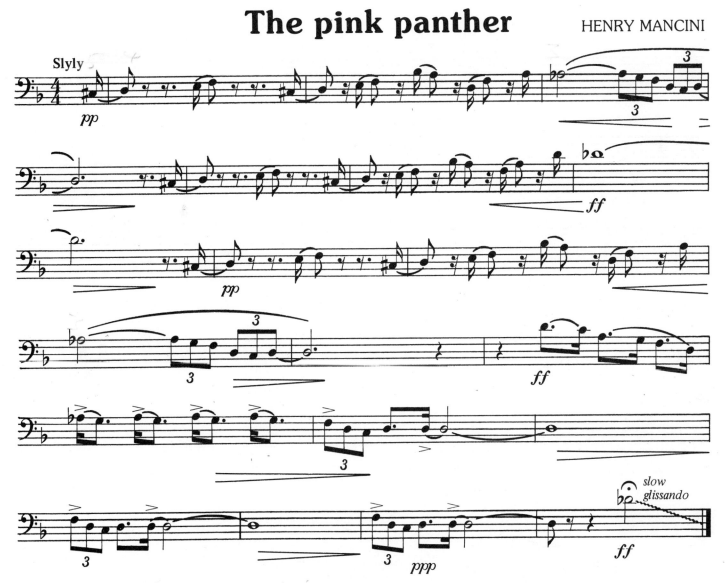

Prometheus theme

LUDWIG VAN BEETHOVEN (1770-1827)

Coronation street

ERIC SPEAR

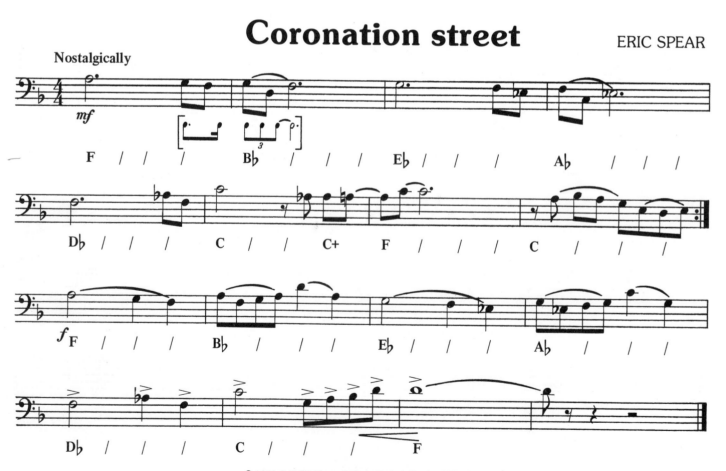

Trumpet march

JEREMIAH CLARKE
(c. 1670-1707)

Theme from Symphony No. 1

JOHANNES BRAHMS (1833-1897)

Little brown jug

Traditional

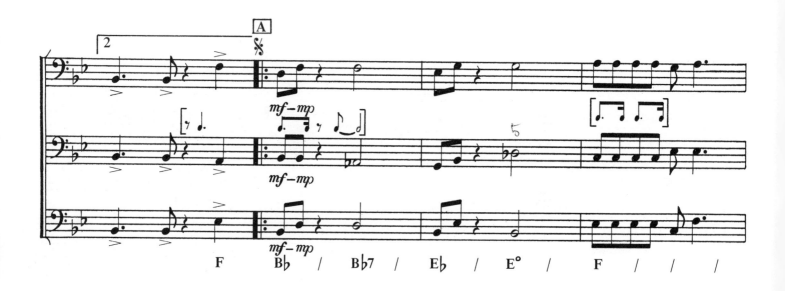

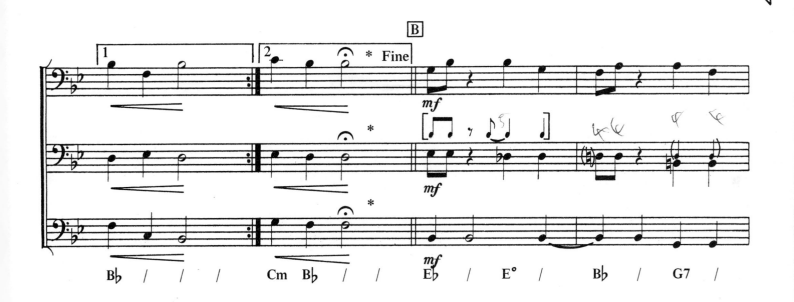

*Improvisation can take place after the 'fine' bar has been played for the first time. Then continue from B and follow signs.

You only live twice

Words by LESLIE BRICUSSE
Music by JOHN BARRY

Superman (theme from)

JOHN WILLIAMS

Dynasty

BILL CONTI

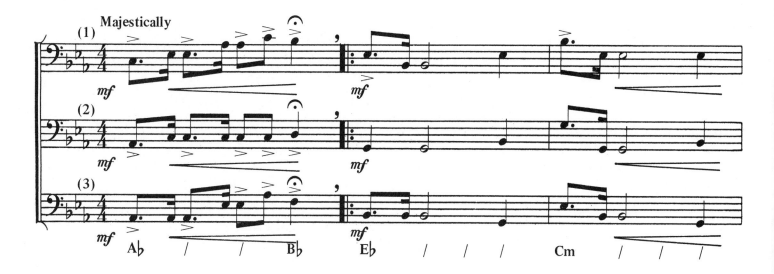

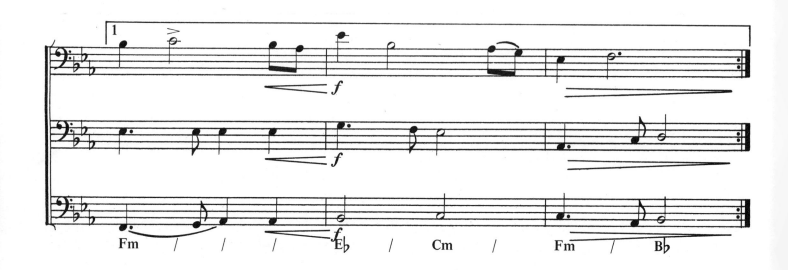

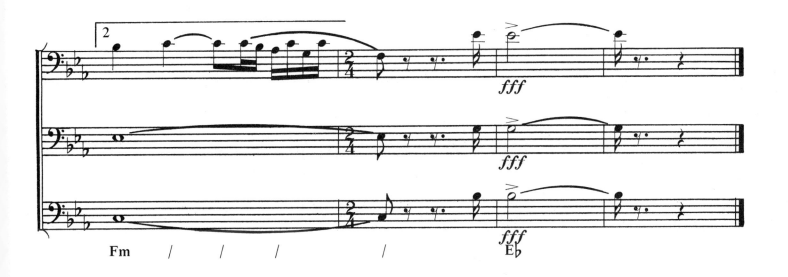

Pomp and circumstance march No. 4

EDWARD ELGAR (1857-1934)

30

The yellow rose of Texas Traditional

© 1990 International Music Publications, Woodford Green, Essex, IG8 8HN.

Farandole

GEORGES BIZET (1838-1875)

© 1990 International Music Publications, Woodford Green, Essex, IG8 8HN.

Match of the day

RHET STOLLER

Printed by
Halstan & Co. Ltd., Amersham, Bucks., England

Index